A Basic Guide To
ARCHERY

An Official U.S. Olympic Committee Sports Series

The U.S. Olympic Committee

Griffin Publishing

Editorial Statement

In the interest of brevity, the Editors have chosen to use the standard English form of address. Please be advised that this usage is not meant to suggest a restriction to, nor an endorsement of, any individual or group of individuals, either by age, gender, or athletic ability. The Editors certainly acknowledge that boys and girls, men and women, of every age and physical condition are actively involved in sports and we encourage everyone to enjoy the sports of his or her choice.

10 9 8 7 6 5 4 3 2 1

ISBN 1-882180-67-4

Griffin Publishing

544 W. Colorado Street
Glendale, California 91204

Telephone: 1-818-244-2128 / Fax 1-818-242-1172

Manufactured in the United States of America

Acknowledgments

PUBLISHER

Robert M. Howland
President, Griffin Publishing

U.S.O.C.

United States Olympic Committee
John Krimsky, Jr.,
Deputy Secretary General

Barry King
Mike Moran
Bob Paul

SERIES EDITOR **Richard D. Burns, Ph.D.**
WRITER **Joey Lorraine Parker**
EDITOR **Suzanne Ledeboer**
BOOK DESIGN **Mark M. Dodge**

NATIONAL ARCHERY **Robert C. Balink**
ASSOCIATION **Jane Johnson**
Christine McCartney
Rick Merriam
Colleen Walker-Mar

EASTON **Don Rabska**
Kathy Velardi

PHOTOS **National Archery Association**
Easton Sports Development Corp.
Lloyd Brown
Leona Perry

COVER DESIGN **L.J. Heart & Associates**

The United States Olympic Committee

The U.S. Olympic Committee (USOC) is the custodian of the U.S. Olympic Movement and is dedicated to providing opportunities for American athletes of all ages.

The USOC, a streamlined organization of member organizations, is the moving force for support of sports in the United States that are on the program of the Olympic and/or Pan American Games, or those wishing to be included.

The USOC has been recognized by the International Olympic Committee since 1894 as the sole agency in the United States whose mission involves training, entering and underwriting the full expenses for the United States teams in the Olympic and Pan American Games. The USOC also supports the bid of U.S. cities to host the winter and summer Olympic Games, or the winter and summer Pan American Games and, after reviewing all the candidates, votes on and may endorse one city per event as the U.S. bid city. The USOC also approves the U.S. trial sites for the Olympic and Pan American Games team selections.

On behalf of the United States Olympic Committee,

Welcome to the Olympic Sports Series

We are extremely pleased to inaugurate the Olympic Sports Series. I feel this unique series will encourage parents, athletes of all ages and novices who are thinking about a sport for the first time, to get involved with the challenging and rewarding world of Olympic sports.

This series of paperback books covers both summer and winter sports, features Olympic history and basic sports fundamentals, and encourages family involvement. Each book includes information on how to get started in a particular sport, including equipment and clothing; rules of the game; health and fitness; basic first aid; and guidelines for spectators. Of special interest is the information on opportunities for senior citizens, volunteers and physically challenged athletes. In addition, each book is enhanced by photographs and illustrations and a complete, easy-to-understand glossary.

Because this family-oriented series neither assumes nor requires prior knowledge of a particular sport, it can be enjoyed by all age groups. Regardless of anyone's level of sports knowledge, playing experience or athletic ability, this official U.S. Olympic Committee Sports Series will encourage understanding and participation in sports and fitness.

The purchase of these books will assist the U.S. Olympic Team. This series supports the Olympic mission and serves importantly to enhance participation in the Olympic and Pan American Games.

John Krimsky, Jr.
Deputy Secretary General

Contents

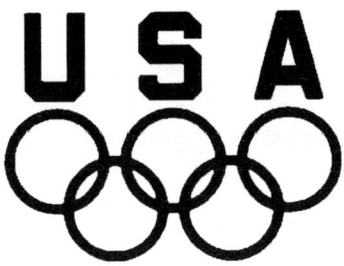

An Athelete's Creed

The most important thing in the Olympic Games is not to win but to take part, just as the most important thing in life is not the triumph but the struggle. The essential thing is not to have conquered but to have fought well.

These famous words, commonly referred to as the Olympic Creed, were once spoken by Baron Pierre de Coubertin, founder of the modern Olympic Games. Whatever their origins, they aptly describe the theme behind each and every Olympic competition.

1

ARCHERY IN THE OLYMPICS

We would be hard pressed to find an athletic endeavor older than archery. Evidence from cave drawings, sandstone sculptures, wood carvings, molded clay figurines, gold, silver and bronze statues, textile weavings, and primitive paintings attests that archery is one of man's oldest, yet most enduring, activities. Moreover, evidence of ancient archery can be found on each of the six populated continents. There are few activities— and even fewer sports—that can boast such historical and worldwide penetration. It is fitting then that we recognize that perhaps no sport in the modern Olympics represents a blending of the old world with the new, the northern hemisphere with the southern, the past with the present, quite as well as archery.

Ancient Archery

As far back as 3500 B.C. the ancient Egyptians used bows almost as tall as the archer, with arrows 2 to 2 1/2 feet long. Arrowheads were first made of flint, then bronze. The King's arrowheads, of course, were made of solid gold.

Artwork abounds depicting man's fascination with archery. This Roman figurine dates to around A.D. 100.

In 1200 B.C., the Hittites of the Middle East developed the highly effective technique of shooting arrows from a moving chariot. Indeed, the Hittites experience is one of the first known attempts at "mobile warfare." Their light, fast chariots allowed them to outmaneuver and outshoot their stationary opponents and to charge into battle at great speed, using the chariot itself as a shield against oncoming arrows, if necessary.

In 1800 B.C., the Assyrians dominated the Middle East with a revolutionary new idea in bow design and construction. Instead of a single piece of wood, they constructed their bows from several different types of material, not only wood but leather, horn and skin, as well. Perhaps the Assyrians' was the first successful compound bow. They also gave the bow a new, recurved shape that was far more powerful than its predecessors and, because it was also shorter, more easily handled by an archer on

The Hittites use of archery from chariots in 1200 B.C. was one of the first effective forms of organized mobile warfare.

horseback. The Assyrians' design in archery equipment opened the door for the attack of the most fierce and famous mounted archers of all: the Mongols led by Attila the Hun.

Middle Eastern superiority in archery equipment and technique continued for centuries. With bows such as those of the Assyrians and Parthians, Attila the Hun and his Mongols conquered much of Europe and Asia, and Turkish archers, using similar equipment, turned back the Crusaders.

Not so fortunate were the Romans of A.D. 100. Though the Romans were—and always have been—considered mighty soldiers, they were only second-rate archers. Until the 5th century their bows were shot by drawing the string only to the chest. Had they used the longer draw to the face, it would have

The Parthians were masters at shooting backward from a galloping horse.

given them the distance and accuracy we know this technique imparts. By A.D. 200, the Romans' opponents—and there were many—were often far better archers, particularly the Parthians, an Asiatic people from the area we now know as northern China. The Parthians were horseman who developed the skill of swiveling around in the saddle and shooting backward, at full gallop. Lightly armored and mounted on swift Arabian horses, they could ride at full speed through enemy ranks, shooting in all directions, and with astounding accuracy!

The Middle Ages

On the European front, the Normans, ex-Vikings from France, used well-sprung longbows which were far superior to the stiff, stubby Saxon bow, as the English woefully learned at the Battle of Hastings in 1066. Norman arrows slew the English King Harold, and the

The most famous of them all: Robin Hood of England

Saxon's defeat helped persuade the English to adopt the longbow as their main weapon.

During the 13th and 14th centuries, English archers came into their own and developed the skill for which they are famous. The respect that the English people held for skilled archers during this time was reflected in the many ballads written about heroic archers. Some of those ballads, such as the Tales of Robin Hood, are still with us today.

Early Tournament Archery

By the 17th century, the invention of gunpowder and lead shot had largely replaced the bow as a weapon of war, but there were still large numbers of trained archers, and interest in the bow and arrow remained strong. In England, regular community festivals involved not just feasting and socializing, but contests which captured the fun and challenge of archery. Archers would compete by shooting arrows at balls tossed in the air, by shooting for distance, or shooting arrows into and through armored shields.

Archers began forming tournaments, and target archery evolved as a competitive sport. One tournament first held in Yorkshire, England, in 1673, the Ancient Scorton Silver Arrow Contest, is still being held today. Women wanted to join men in archery competitions and in 1787 the Royal British Bowmen became the first archery society to admit women.

In the United States, the Civil War was partly responsible for the rise in interest in archery. After the war, men who had been Confederate soldiers were not permitted to use firearms. Two veterans, brothers Will and Maurice Thompson, decided to carve out a new life for themselves in the wilderness, and with the help of Indians in Florida, they trained themselves in archery. Maurice Thompson's book, *The Witchery of Archery*, captured their love of the sport. The book was widely read and interest in target archery spread rapidly across the United States and Canada.

The National Archery Association (NAA) was founded—and held its first tournament—in Chicago in 1879. To no one's surprise, Will Thompson won, then went on to win the next five national tournaments.

Two Eras in Olympic Archery

Although the ancient Olympics are alleged to have been founded by an archer—Hercules, the mythical hero of the ancient Greeks—archery didn't become an official event in the modern Olympics until the Olympiad at Paris in 1900. The tradition of friendship and good times of the 18th century English tournaments was carried on in this world-class archery competition.

The Olympic Committee had no standard rules to go by, so they tried to accommodate the different countries' styles and rules. For example, they included an event called *la perche*, or the "popinjay." The targets in popinjay are bright colored "birds" made of feathers wrapped around a cotton base, tied to the top of a mast. A special blunt head is added to the arrows so as not to damage the popinjay target. Although popinjay remains popular in Europe, especially in Belgium, it is no longer part of the Olympic archery program. The French walked away with the honors in that first modern Olympiad—they won three medals, Belgium two, and Australia one.

Photo courtesy of NAA

Women's archery event at the 1908 Games in London.

The Olympic Games of 1904, held in St. Louis, also included an archery event, but it was poorly attended. American archers took all the honors, but in truth, they had little competition. In 1904, few countries could afford to send teams by steamship all the way to America.

Archery competition at the 1908 Olympic Games in London saw the inclusion of women's events. The Royal Toxophilite Society, the governing body of archery in England, set the rules for the competitors which included 25 women and 15 men from Great Britain; 11 men from France; and 1 man from the United States—H. G. Richardson, the reigning U.S. Champion. The rules committee concerned itself with more than just the scoring of rounds. Manners on the field were a primary concern and strictly governed by the RTS. This is hardly surprising

Photo courtesy of NAA

During the Edwardian era, archery was a popular pastime of the aristocracy, and one of the few sports "socially acceptable" for ladies. In this 1903 photo, English Ladies Champion, Alice B. Legh shows good form on the follow through.

considering that this was the height of the Edwardian Era, a time of opulent excess when manners and behavior were often viewed as more important than final results. Great Britain took 6 medals that year, France 4, and H. G. Richardson, the lone American entry, went home with a Bronze.

There was no archery competition at the 1912 Olympic Games in Stockholm, Sweden, and, because of World War I, there were no Games held in 1916. Therefore, archery did not reappear until the 1920 Olympics in Antwerp, Belgium. As was the practice with many sports, the host country set up the rules for a sport according to how it was played in the host's country. Belgium decided to make popinjay— a target game popular in Belgium—a major event. Not surprisingly, Belgium won 6 medals, with The Netherlands, France and England taking one medal each. Unfortunately, largely due to a lack of consistent rules, archery began to flounder as an international competitive sport. After 1920, its place in Olympic competition appeared bleak.

Modern Olympic Archery

For international archery to survive, universal rules had to be established. The breakthrough came in the 1930s when Poland hosted the first real international archery contest and helped to organize the Fédération Internationale de Tir a l'Arc (FITA), the

International Archery Federation. Today, FITA is the central governing body for international archery competition.

By the 1972 Olympic Games in Munich, Germany, FITA rules were recognized and firmly established throughout the world, and the "FITA Round" was adopted for Olympic competition. In the single FITA round, male competitors shoot 36 arrows (6 sets of 6 arrows) from distances of 90, 70, 50, and 30 meters. Women shoot 36 arrows (6 sets of 6 arrows) from distances of 70, 60, 50, and 30 meters. After each set of 6 arrows, the archers record their scores and retrieve their arrows. For Olympic competition a double FITA round is shot: 72 arrows from the same distances.

During the 1972 Olympics, John Williams, an 18-year-old American, took the gold in the men's double FITA round, scoring 2,528 out of a possible 2,880. Another American, Doreen Wilber, took the gold in the women's double FITA round. Doreen Wilber established a new world record by shooting a score of 2,424.

The 1976 Olympics in Montreal, Canada, brought together men and women archers from 25 countries. By the end of the event, each of the competitors had shot round, scoring 1,282 points out of a possible 1,440, 288 arrows over 4 days of very tough competition. Darrell Pace, the American national champion of 1975, broke Olympic records in winning the gold medal in 1976. Also in Montreal, American Luann Ryon won the gold and set a new Olympic and world record for the women's single FITA round, scoring 1,282 points out of a possible 1,440.

For political reasons, the United States did not attend the 1980 Olympic Games in Moscow, but American archers were well prepared and ready to defend their titles at the 1984 Games in Los Angeles. Darrel Pace, who had won a gold medal in Montreal in 1976 repeated his brilliant performance and captured another gold in 1984.

At the 1988 Olympic Games in Seoul, Korea, a new dimension was added to archery with the advent of the team competition. American Jay Barrs won the men's individual gold medal, then, along with Rick McKinney and Darrel Pace, captured the team silver. The U. S. women's team consisting of Denise Parker, Debra Ochs and Melanie Skillman, won a hard-fought bronze medal. United States archers were again shooting well at the 1992 Olympics in Barcelona, Spain, and both the men's and women's teams get stronger and more competitive every year.

National Archery Association (NAA)

The National Archery Association of the United States was formed in 1879 to foster and promote the

Photo courtesy of Leona Perry

The NAA's College Program enables archers such as 19-year-old Vic Wunderle to compete while attending school. Vic won three golds and one silver at the 1995 Pan American Games.

sport of archery through tournaments, programs and publications. The NAA is a member of the U.S. Olympic Committee and the National Governing Body for the sport of archery in the United States. The NAA conducts tournaments, oversees instructional clinics, maintains records, and provides organized archery clubs throughout the country with a well-rounded program of events. As the official sanctioning body, the NAA selects archery teams to represent the United States in Olympic and Pan American Games, and also selects teams for Target, Field and Indoor archery in World Championship events.

Junior Olympic Archery Development (JOAD)

In the early 1960s the National Archery Association of the United States recognized a need for an archery development program specifically for young archers. To fulfill that need, the Junior Olympic Archery Development (JOAD) program was established in 1961, and has shown steady and continuous growth ever since. The purpose of the program is to provide a basic organizational guide for junior archery activities. The NAA, with its Olympic membership affiliation, is the guiding force for these potential Olympic and international archery contestants. The program is also intended to provide the necessary guidance for the recreational archer who is interested in archery purely for the enjoyment of shooting a bow and arrow.

Photo courtesy of Lloyd Brown

The JOAD program enables young archers to make new friends and have fun. These happy fellows competed successfully at the U.S. Target Championships in 1994.

Membership is open to any boy or girl, age 18 and under—the only requirement is that you have an interest in archery. A club can be chartered under the NAA when an adult leader, with three or more archers, makes an application to the National Archery Association. If you and your friends have an interest in archery, ask a responsible adult to be your group's supervisor, then apply for official NAA club status. The NAA offers instructional assistance

Photo courtesy of Leona Perry

Three-time World Champion USA's Rick McKinney at the 1995 Pan American Games.

for your group supervisor, and all club members will have the benefit of being able to participate in NAA-sanctioned archery events. As your skill improves you will be eligible to earn NAA official Ranking Certificates, Classification Patches and Medal Classification Bars. All are displayed with great pride by those members fortunate enough to earn them.

The College Division Program

The College Division Program is for archers who are full-time students at campuses with official archery clubs. Full-time students may apply for tuition assistance through the NAA's Scholarship Fund program. The NAA can advise you of which U.S. colleges and universities offer a sanctioned archery program.

U.S. Archery Team (USAT)

The NAA sponsors the U.S. Archery Team. *Junior USAT* and *Compound USAT* are for national and international competition. Members for both men's and women's teams are chosen from rankings earned at selected NAA tournaments. Training camps are held for USAT and other NAA-approved archery teams. One of the most prestigious spots is to be selected for the Resident Athlete Program at the U.S. Olympic Committee's ARCO Training Center. This program focuses on developing archers for national and international competition with daily state-of-the-art physical and psychological conditioning.

2

ARCHERY COMPETITIONS

One of the great benefits of archery is that people can enjoy this sport at almost any age. Children as young as seven can draw a traditional bow and adults well into their eighties can be found on the range, either target or field. Moreover, archery offers a variety of ways to participate. Most people start with target archery as that is the best place to learn the fundamentals of shooting, but if you are a person who enjoys getting back to nature and welcomes a hike through the woods, field archery may be your ultimate goal. Want to try something different? Have you ever tried shooting 18 holes on a beautiful golf course? But have you tried it with bow and arrows, instead of golf clubs? Now you've got to admit, that's different! Archery golf, clout shooting, and flight archery definitely appeal to those seeking the unusual. In this chapter, we'll take a look at these and other archery activities, everything from the very traditional to the extreme. Try them all to find the one that best meets *your* needs.

Target Archery

Probably the most common and best-known form of archery is target archery. Even people who have never shot a bow don't have to ask what sport is being played when they see the colorful target faces set up in a field.

Target faces are very distinctive and must conform to a standard design and color scheme. Working from the center outward, the colors are: gold, red, light blue, black, and white. Each color is divided by a thin line into two zones of equal width. Both zones of the same color have equal scoring value. In its entirety, a target face has 10 scoring zones of equal width, measured from the center of the target.

Competitors using different types of bows are grouped into separate divisions and compete in separate events. The FITA-approved divisions for outdoor target archery are: (1) Olympic Division; (2) Standard Bow Division; and (3) Compound Division. For indoor target archery, only Olympic and Compound are used.

If you are a beginning archer aspiring to organized competition, remember that not all tackle and/or accessories are acceptable for all events, divisions, and rounds. Refer to the FITA or NAA Rule Book to be sure your equipment is authorized for the type of competition you want to enter. It would be terrible to shoot a good score and then have it disqualified for having used an unauthorized piece of equipment. To explain this further, let's take a look at the type of equipment allowed for the FITA-sanctioned Olympic Division of outdoor target archery.

Olympic Division

Recurve bows are the choice of most Olympic archers, and take-down bows are also acceptable. A take-down bow is one in which the limbs can be removed from the handle when the bow is not in use. The bowstring may be composed of any number of strands, but it may not have sight markings, a peephole, or any other aids which could influence the archer's aim. Arrowrests and clickers may be used, but they too must be devoid of aiming devices. Bowsights and stabilizers are permitted, but must conform to FITA-approved standards.

Any type of approved target arrows may be used. The arrows of each archer must be marked on the shaft with the competitor's name or initials, and all of an archer's arrows must carry the same pattern and colors of fletching, nocks, and cresting. This, of course, aids in score keeping and identifying the arrows of each competitor.

Finger tabs or three-finger shooting gloves are permitted, but mechanical release aids are not. In addition, some archers prefer to use an anchor plate. This device is worn in the drawing hand and helps the archer position his or her shooting hand prior to the release. Anchor plates are permitted in the Olympic Division. Scopes, field glasses, shooting glasses and other such arrow-spotting devices are permitted, but must not be marked in any way that could influence aim. The non-sighting eye may be covered or an eye patch may be worn.

Additional accessories such as arm guard, clothing shield, bowsling, belt or ground quiver (where arrows are kept upright in a metal quiver stuck in the ground), rub rag (called a tassel), and foot markers (to aid in placing the feet for the stance) are all permitted. No other devices or accessories are allowed.

This gives you an idea of the type of equipment target archers use in the Olympic Division of international competitions. For complete details about the type of contest you want to enter, or to learn more about Olympic and other competitive divisions, consult the FITA or NAA Rule Book.

Field Archery

Field archery developed when a group of bowhunters realized that if they were to perfect their hunting techniques, they needed to practice in a more natural setting. The manicured lawns and pre-determined distances of target shooting were not thorough enough training for hunting when one never knows where game will appear, nor at what distance. To that end, the National Field Archery Association (NFAA) was formed in California in 1939. Since then, the organization has become a federation and governing body of state field archery groups throughout the United States, each group consisting of the field archery clubs within each state.

The concept of field archery ranges, also called courses, developed as a direct result of pioneer field archers roaming the hills and woods, shooting at inanimate objects from various angles and distances. This type of practice, they felt, was far more practical. It wasn't long before field archery courses were being laid out all over the country—and even today, more people participate in field archery than in any other type of organized archery.

But field archery, too, has undergone changes. Most notably, no longer is field archery composed mostly of bowhunters. Nowadays most NFAA members are more interested in field archery tournaments than they are with learning how to hunt. In the early stages, all field archers shot with the same tackle used in bowhunting. But with today's greater emphasis on high scores, most tournament winners have changed to lighter bows and arrows, and the general members are following suit. Even so, the NFAA still offers a bowhunter membership classification and maintains an educational Bowhunting and Conservation Committee.

FITA Field Archery Round

The *Federation Internationale de Tir a l'Arc* sponsors a field round that is being shot in most countries. The FITA Field Round has three divisions: barebow, freestyle and compound. Within each division, there are two classes according to gender for a total of six classifications. Rules are quite explicit with regard to the equipment used in each division. Barebow shooters are not permitted any aids for estimating distance. That means sights, markings on the upper bow limb (draw-check indicators) are not permitted. The bow must be completely bare, without any protrusions, marks, blemishes or laminated pieces.

The freestyle division does allow adjustable arrow rests, clickers, bow sights and stabilizers on the bow. Unlike barebow, telescopes and other visual aids may be used in this division.

If you are using a compound bow, the draw weight may not exceed sixty pounds. It may have the equipment allowed in the freestyle division. In addition, peep-sights, levels and release aids are permitted. Target distances range from 5 to 60 meters. Twelve targets make up a unit, and twice through the course constitutes a field round. The distances for an unmarked course are slightly shorter than for a marked course. The unit for the Finals Round has 8 targets with half of the targets marked and other half unmarked distances.

Target faces are 20 centimeters in diameter for the shorter distances and up to 80 centimeters for the longest 3 targets. The background of the target face is white, with the first and third rings from the outside gray. The second and fourth rings are black and the center spot is white. The scoring value points are, ranging from the inside to the outside, 5, 4, 3, 2, and 1.

An official FITA Field Round consists of 72 arrows, 3 per target on 24 targets for a perfect score of 360 points.

NFAA Field Round

The National Field Archery Association (NFAA) of the United States is the umbrella organization located in Redlands, California. The primary goal of the NFAA is to provide a framework by which state, regional and local associations may become affiliated with a national body. The NFAA is an excellent source for information about field archery and this resource is always available to members. For more information, contact the NFAA (see page 29).

NFAA Classifications

The NFAA has several classifications for shooting according to age, gender, equipment and division. The equipment categories are governed by the type of bow and whether a release aid is used or not. The competitive bowhunter division is for archers using heavy hunting-type tackle. As with the barebow division, the competitive bowhunter is not allowed to use a sight or a release aid. They basically use their instinctive abilities to hit the target.

Two other classes are the freestyle and the freestyle limited. Sights and stabilizers may be used on the bows for both styles, however, the limited class may not use a release aid.

Classifications are further divided by age and gender. Cub division is for children 11 and under. Youth division covers ages 12-14, and youth adult division for teens 15-17. Adult division for men and women, ages 18-54, and senior adult division for those 55 and over. In the adult division, there are professional and amateur classifications. Professionals are eligible to receive monetary awards in sanctioned tournaments. The NFAA also sponsors a national ranking system that allows the professional archers to earn ranking points in national, sectional and state championships.

The NFAA has established a handicap that may be used in local, state and national competition. It is a point system that provides a fair handicap for all archers regardless of ability.

NFAA Rounds

The NFAA sponsors several indoor and outdoor rounds. They vary in distances, type of target face, number of arrows, positions, and scoring. There are generally 14 targets situated in the woods and twice through is a field round. The target faces vary in size from 35 centimeters to 65 centimeters. Four arrows are shot at each target, generally from the same stake. Four targets, however, are shot either from 4 different stakes or from 1 stake at 4 separate target faces. The archer may also shoot one arrow from each of 4 stakes at either 2 or 4 target faces.

The field target face is black and white alternating rings. The Hunter Round is an all black face with a white spot. Pictures of animals with scoring areas are used for the Animal Round. The NFAA International Round, 810 Target Round and the 900 Target Round are designed mostly for open field shooting. Olympic-style FITA multicolored faces are used for the 810 and 900 Target Rounds.

Some clubs have facilities for indoor rounds and this is especially nice when weather turns bad. Also, many regular indoor target ranges allow field clubs to set up field targets and shoot indoors.

The indoor rounds utilize target faces of various sizes and designs. With the exception of the Flint Bowman Indoor Round, the shooting line is 20 yards from the mats. A blue and white target face with scoring points counted from inside to outside as 5, 4, 3, 2, and 1 is used for the Indoor, Championship and Freeman Rounds. Animal faces are used for the Bowhunter Round.

Archery Golf

For maximum fun, shoot this on a real golf course. The objective is to shoot 18 holes with the fewest shots. Archers "tee-off" with shots down the fairway. As they approach the tee, they count the number of shots as golfers record strokes. Any weight or type of bow is permitted, and any type of arrow. There is, however, a real "science" to successful archery golf. Some archery golfers use a flight arrow for the tee shot to get maximum distance, a target arrow for the fairway, a flu-flu arrow for the approach and either a target arrow or a flu-flu for the "putt." A full or partial draw is permissible.

A ball, 4 inches in diameter, is placed on a metal wire on the green. The archers must hit the ball with the arrow. The ball must be shot or knocked off the stand to "hole-out." If the approach shot is so close that the archer can stand with both feet behind the spot where the arrow landed and touch the ball with a nocked arrow, it is a successful putt.

If you shoot archery golf in a large field (as opposed to on a real golf course), you may have a time finding stray arrows. One solution is to shoot in pairs. Have your partner follow the flight of your arrow, and you do the same for your partner.

For everyone's safety, approach archery golf as seriously as you would regular golf. All archers and spectators should stay well behind the person shooting, and make sure anyone on the course ahead of you is well out of range before you (or anyone in your group) takes a shot.

Clout Shooting

National clout shooting championships are held each year as an addition to the NAA's National Outdoor Target Championships. An interesting round, it may be adapted to the equipment of the class. The longest official distance is 165 meters for men, and 125 meters for women. In clout shooting, the bullseye is laid out on the ground and marked by a flag (the "clout"). A flag is put in the center of the scoring area, with a stake below the center of the flag to which a 25 1/2-foot chain is attached. The chain is used for scoring. The chain is marked off as follows: closest to the stake, gold; then red, blue, black, white, and clear out on the free end. Each color section is 4 ft., 3 in. long.

Once the arrows have been shot, one end of the chain is attached to the stake and the chain is stretched to full length. With the chain stretched taut and held close to the ground, the person holding the free end walks one full circle around the stake. Score keepers walk behind the chain as it makes its revolution, pulling arrows out of the appropriate scoring area. Once all arrows have been picked up, they are grouped by crest and laid on the color of the scoring area that represents where they landed. As each archer's name is called, he retrieves his arrows (identifying them by crest) and calls out his score, from highest to lowest in scoring values.

Flight Archery

Flight archery is just what the name implies; the object is to shoot an arrow as far as it will go. Flight archery appeals especially to those with a keen interest in math, science and engineering in that successful shooting takes knowledge of trajectories and aerodynamics.

Competitions in flight shooting are divided into three classes: target bows, flight bows (much shorter and more powerful), and freestyle bows. The freestyle class is most amusing to watch as many of the archers choose to lie on their backs and rest their bows on their feet.

Legend has it that a certain 18th century Turkish Sultan shot an arrow 972 yards. It took 200 years to beat his record, but American freestyle archer Harry Drake is reported to have shot an arrow 1,100 yards. Do you think you can beat that? Hint: Before trying a flight-for-distance shot, make sure you are shooting over a wide open field. Never shoot where an arrow can come down in a populated area.

Wand Shoot

While you may not set any distance records, the wand shoot is something you can set up even in your own backyard. Take a 3-inch wide strip of masking tape and stick it vertically along the target butt. At 20 meters or more, 24 arrows are shot at the "wand." Arrows that pierce the tape earn 5 points. In the standard Wand Round, 36 arrows are shot from 60 yards at a 2-in. x 6-ft. piece of soft wood such as balsa or pine.

Archery Associations & Governing Bodies

Bowhunters of America (BOA)
1030 W. Central Avenue
Bismark, North Dakota 58501

Fédération Internationale de Tir a l'Arc (FITA)
(International Archery Federation)
Via Bartolini 39
Milan, Italy

International Bowhunting Organization (IBO)
P. O. Box 8564
Middletown, Ohio 45042

Junior Olympic Archery Development Program (JOAD)
A Youth-oriented Division of the NAA
One Olympic Plaza
Colorado Springs, Colorado 80909
(719) 578-4576

National Archery Association (NAA) of the United States
One Olympic Plaza
Colorado Springs, Colorado 80909
(719) 578-4576

> *The NAA is the target archers' organization and the official governing body for the sport of archery in the United States. Affiliated with FITA, the NAA is the United States' link with the Olympic Games*

National Field Archery Association (NFAA)
31407 Outer I-10
Redlands, California 92373

Professional Archers Association (PAA)
26 Lakeview Drive
Stansbury Park, Utah 84704

3

TACKLE & EQUIPMENT

While it's true that Olympic archers use very sophisticated equipment, one of the nicest things about archery is that you can get started with just a few basics. It's not necessary to have every option and accessory for your first attempt. Start with a simple bow and some inexpensive arrows. A bale of straw (purchased at a feed store) makes a fine backyard target. Later, you may want to upgrade your tackle as your shooting improves, and you will be better able to make sound buying decisions if you know what type of equipment would best meet your needs. In this chapter, we'll take a look at different bows and arrows and how they are used.

Bows and Strings

Traditional Bow

A suitable and cost-effective bow for learning is the traditional (or straight) bow. Quite simply, a traditional bow is unadorned and shaped in the

Photo courtesy of NAA

Shooting a traditional bow is an excellent way to
learn the basics. This young archer is smartly turned
out in her JOAD club attire and is giving this shot
her full concentration.

form of an arc. Some clubs have bows you can use, but you may wish to purchase your own. Arrows will need to be purchased separately. In all fairness, this type of bow will not give you the pinpoint accuracy and speed of a composite or recurve bow, but don't let that put you off. You can have a lot of fun with a traditional bow without having to make a big investment. You can always upgrade to more sophisticated equipment when you are ready.

Composite Bow

Basically, a composite bow is any bow constructed of two or more fabrics which are joined together. The fabrics most often used today are wood and fiberglass, although some bows incorporate very lightweight aluminum into their overall design. Melding two or more materials gives a bow added strength, flexibility, and resilience. The post-World War II invention and application of lightweight materials such as fiberglass and aluminum have lessened the weight while increasing the strength and power. Most bows today, unless they are custom made out of wood by choice, are going to be some type of composite. If you see a bow you would like to purchase, be sure to ask what materials were used to manufacture the bow, and of what percentages. This information will help you select the proper arrows for that particular bow. Also, bowstrings come in various thicknesses, depending on the number of strands in the string. Your archery tackle shop can advise you on the most suitable bowstring for any bow you select.

The tips of the bows shown in this photo curve up and out. These are "recurve" bows.

Recurve Bow

Recurve bows were re-invented shortly after World War II. We say re-invented because the ancient Turks had a version of the recurve bow as early as the 12th century, but the recurve bow as we think of it today was developed in the late 1940s and early 1950s. Of course design and composition continue to change, but modern recurve bows have their roots in the post-WW II era. A popular choice with top archers is fiberglass laminated in two layers with an inner core of hardwood. This gives the bow "spring," and the recurve tips allow for greater storage and release of energy than could be found in a non-recurve bow. If you are thinking of purchasing a bow, a good choice is one that is laminated, center shot, and has working recurves.

Take-Down Bow

A take-down bow is just what the name implies— the limbs can be detached from the handle when the bow is not in use. Take down bows have two distinct advantages: (1) they are easier to transport and store, and (2) they allow you to purchase new limbs instead of having to buy a complete new bow when you are able to draw more weight. Also, if you enjoy both target and field archery, you can simply snap in the appropriate limbs for the type of arrows you'll

Photo courtesy of NAA

**These archers are shooting compound bows. Note the
pulleys and cables connecting the limbs.**

be shooting. The downside, if there is one, is that
they are considerably more expensive to buy initially.
Let your needs and your budget be your guide.

Compound Bow

Compound bows are especially popular with
hunters and field archers because, thanks to a
complex setup of pulleys and cables, they are easier
to hold at full draw than a recurve bow would be.
The main pulleys on the ends of the bow are mounted
eccentrically; the axle of the pulley is off center.
When an archer pulls back the string of a compound

bow with a 40-pound draw weight, he or she initially draws 40 pounds. But when the string is approximately halfway drawn, the eccentric pulleys flip over and absorb a good percentage of that weight, roughly about half as much. So, after the initial draw, it requires only about 20 pounds of the archer's energy to hold the bow at full draw.

Moreover, when the arrow is released, its initial thrust has 20 pounds behind it, but by the time the shaft leaves the bow, it takes off with a 40-pound thrust. This is the polar opposite of what happens to an arrow shot from a traditional or recurve bow; it loses velocity immediately after the release. Arrows shot from compound bows actually gain speed, which is one reason they are so popular with hunters.

Flight Bows

If ever there was a purpose-built item it was the flight bow. Shorter, stiffer and much more powerful than its fellow target and field bows, the flight bow is used solely for distance shooting. In truth, a flight bow is not a good choice for a beginner. You will be limited to shooting only for distance, and there are not that many places you can compete even in the distance shoot. You will have more opportunities with a traditional, recurve or compound bow, but that is not to suggest that distance shooting couldn't be a component of your overall archery experience.

Crossbow

Today the crossbow is a popular sporting device, but it has a long history as a weapon both for hunting and for warfare. The Chinese seem to have been the first to use the crossbow, and historical records indicate they made and successfully operated crossbows as early as 700 B.C. Our most complete information, however, comes from the Han Dynasty which lasted from 206 B.C to A.D. 220. Historical documents from that era report crossbows with draw weights of 190 to 380 pounds!

It is uncertain when the crossbow passed from Asia to Europe. The Romans used a type of crossbow around the time of King Constantine (A.D. 272-337) and some records indicate that a crossbow was used in central Europe early in the 11th century. But no matter how humble its early origin, in our mind's eye the crossbow forever will be associated with the Crusades of the 12th century. A knight in shinning armor, crossbow at the ready, mounted on a gleaming horse bedecked with the heraldry of its master's home court—these images are rich and long lasting. In fact, during the Crusades, crossbow warfare became so grizzly that in 1139 Pope Innocent II made it illegal to carry a crossbow. He deemed that they were too violent and destructive, and anyone caught with one (at least within the city limits of Constantinople) would have it confiscated.

By 1415 records show only 38 crossbowmen listed in the army of King Henry V of England. Even though the use of the crossbow was declining in England, it was in common use in the European campaigns until around 1500. At this time in the newly discovered Western Hemisphere, *Generalissimo Hernando Cortez de España* had a company of crossbowmen in the army when he invaded Mexico in 1521.

In the 16th century, laws were passed in England against the use of the crossbow, except by certain foresters who were allowed to use it to kill game. As a result, crossbow shooting became a sporting activity of noblemen and the leisure class. Guilds were formed and target archery with the crossbow became very popular.

The crossbow had an advantage over the longbow in that it could be held in the drawn position for a longer period of time. By contrast, an archer with a longbow would soon tire. Even so, the heavy crossbow used in warfare had distinct disadvantages: it was cumbersome, expensive, had a slow rate of fire, and was difficult to draw. In fact, as the crossbow became more powerful, its difficulties increased right along with the power. It was at this time that numerous mechanical devices were invented to aid in cocking, most to little or no avail.

Over the centuries, of course, most of the early difficulties have been eliminated, thanks to the invention of lightweight yet strong materials such as fiberglass, and to better hardware. The target crossbow today consists of a set of small limbs (called a prod) which are usually made of fiberglass or, more commonly, wood-fiberglass lamination. The prod is mounted on a wooden gunstock. The combined length of the limbs when strung must not exceed 36 inches. The bolt, as the crossbow arrow is called, must not exceed 15 inches and may be made of aluminum, fiberglass, or wood. The bolts are usually fletched with very small feathers.

The crossbow is usually cocked by placing a foot in a stirrup at the front end of the stock, and drawing the string back to the split-trigger, which will hold the string in a full drawn position until the trigger is squeezed. In shooting, the crossbow is held in a manner similar to a rifle.

There is national competition with the crossbow, as there is a crossbow division with the NAA. The rules for shooting with a crossbow are the same for the longbow, except that the target face is smaller. For example, the crossbow division has a 900 round that is identical to the longbow round, except that a 60 cm. target is used instead of the 122 cm. (48-in.) target face.

The crossbowmen have done much to preserve the heraldry in archery and in doing so have created an interesting and colorful spectator and participant sport. If possible, go out and watch a crossbow competition. You will find it fascinating and enjoyable, and may even end up wanting to add the crossbow to your other archery ventures.

Whichever type of shooting you decide to do, make the bow, not the arrows, your first purchase. You need to select a bow that not only meets your shooting needs, but one that fits your body. After you have selected a bow, then purchase arrows that are complementary to your bow. In the next section we'll look at the types of arrows you'll want to consider.

Arrows

Four major types of arrows are on the market today: wood, fiberglass, aluminum, and aluminum-carbon. Fletching is most readily available in either feathers or plastic vanes. Each arrow composition has its own characteristics and performs differently, even when shot from the same bow.

The shaft and length must be considered when purchasing arrows. Your draw length and peak bow weight determine which of the various arrow shaft sizes is best, since the length of the arrow will change the spine of any particular shaft size. Arrows of an improper length—relative to your draw— won't fly well out of the bow. Moreover, you don't need to be off by a mile to notice the difference. An arrow even one-inch shorter or longer that it should be will adversely affect your accuracy. So the selection of arrows is important.

The most accurate way of determining draw length is by pulling an arrow marked in inches. A good archery tackle shop will have a measuring arrow available, and it is always a good idea to let experienced personnel help you. It's hard to measure yourself accurately. Beginning archers should select an arrow length that extends 2 inches beyond the back of the bow. (Remember, the back of the bow is the side facing the *target*.) This safety margin will reduce the possibility of an overdraw and subsequent injury. Once the length of the arrow and the poundage of the bow are determined, select the arrow size by referring to a manufacturer's spine chart. Again, your tackle shop will help you with this. If possible, try a few arrows of that length before purchasing. Some shops have a collection of arrows of various sizes you can try right in the shop. Don't worry about scoring a bullseye or trying to impress the sales clerk, concentrate on what you're there for. Your objective is to determine the proper arrow length for you. Take advantage of that opportunity.

Once you have determined the appropriate length, it's time to consider arrow composition. Two factors are most prevalent in this decision: (1) the type of shooting you want to do, and (2) your budget.

Wood

Wood arrows are the least expensive, but also the least durable. Even in normal use they can warp, particular in humid or very damp areas of the country. They cannot be as closely matched as the other compositions and, as a result, may give erratic results, but they are an inexpensive way to get started. Consider also that if you are a beginner, your accuracy probably isn't all that exact yet anyway, hence the slight fluctuation in flight at this point isn't that important. If wood arrows are what your budget allows, then get them. After all, at this stage in the game it's more important to get started arching than to fret over arrow composition.

Fiberglass

Fiberglass is another good choice for beginners. The cost is reasonable, they are more durable than wood, and they can be better fitted to your draw length and bow weight. The biggest drawback is that fiberglass is considerably heavier than aluminum, and if you have lightweight tackle you may find that fiberglass arrows have trouble reaching the longer distances. You won't know for sure until you have shot a few.

Aluminum

For recreational shooting, aluminum is perhaps the best all-around arrow on the market today. Aluminum arrows are more consistent in spine and weight than either wood or fiberglass, and they are manufactured with various outside diameters and wall thicknesses. Aluminum arrows have also found favor with hunters and field archers. Should they hit a rock or get wet, their durability reduces the risk of breaks and cracks.

Aluminum-Carbon

Now you're in the high-rent district. The aluminum-carbon shaft is the most advanced product in arrow production today. Its superior performance has been proven by advanced archers throughout the world. Several national and international records have been broken with aluminum-carbon arrows.

The core of the arrow is a precision drawn, high strength aluminum tube. Carbon fibers are bonded to the aluminum core. This increases the strength of the core, allowing the shaft to be much smaller and lighter.

Another high-tech arrow shaft is the seamless carbon composite tube. They are lightweight and smaller in diameter than aluminum arrows. They are for advanced competitive archers and are the arrow of choice of Olympic and other world-class shooters. Shaft stiffness causes archers to spend hours tuning their bows. That, and their very high cost, makes them an inadvisable choice for all but tip-top archers. You don't need to spend that kind of money to get started. In all honesty, the beauty and performance ability of the equipment is beyond you at this point. Outfitting yourself with these arrows for your first day on the range would be akin to turning someone loose in a Ferrari who had never driven before in his life. You need only realize that high-tech equipment does exist and that it will be there for you when you are ready.

Fletching

The type of fletching for arrows is largely a matter of personal preference, but again, the type of shooting you plan to do must be considered. Hunters who can get close to their prey, prefer "flu-flu" arrows. Flu-flus have more than three rows of fletching. The extra fletching puts wind resistance on the arrow and keeps it from traveling too far. By contrast, plastic vanes are the fletching of choice for outdoor target archers and most field archers. The plastic vanes produce the least amount of wind resistance and are not affected by rain, snow or humidity. Feathers (specifically turkey feathers) are the traditional fletching, and archers often prefer them when shooting indoors.

Targets

When used conversationally, the word "target" has a bit of a double meaning. The target itself is the exact thing you are shooting at, be it a field target or a traditional circular target, the latter is officially called the "target face." The material behind the target face—the material which absorbs the arrow—

is the "target backstop" or "target butt." In conversation, *face* and *backstop* are often run together and referred to collectively as "the target."

Target Butts

Almost any strong yet absorbent material can be used as a backstop, the most common being baled straw or hay. More sophisticated backstops are the circular woven mats used at official target archery events. These mats are made of a special type of cord grass known as Indian grass. The grass is tightly woven, then covered with burlap. The strong burlap cover is then sewn onto the woven mat with 300-pound-test rot-resistant polypropylene twine. Once it's on, that burlap cover is not going anywhere! The most expensive and best made mats have a further-reinforced section in the center, the area that (hopefully) gets the greatest wear. Woven mats come in various sizes, ranging from the smallest at 16-in. in diameter to the largest at 48-in. in diameter. The 48-inch size is the FITA and NAA regulation size for all official target archery competition.

Target Faces

Several target faces are used in different styles of shooting. Target faces used in competitions must conform to the standards set by the various governing bodies, so if you plan on doing any competitive shooting, you probably should practice on official-looking target faces. That way you'll be familiar with the target face you'll see in the tournament and will have had a chance to adjust your aim for that target face. The Olympic Games use the traditional multi-colored face of concentric rings, but other colors and patterns are used in other competitions.

If you buy a target face, try to get one that has been treated with a transparent protective coating. They are a little more expensive than plain paper, but will last much longer. Paper target faces are the least expensive and most readily available, but paper tears in no time at all. If the arrows don't get it, the wind surely will. If you buy a plain paper target face, mount it onto cardboard first, then attach the cardboard to the target butt. Be sure to take it in when you have finished shooting.

All pretreated target faces last longer and may well prove to be the better buy. Reinforced faces are made with hundreds of nylon threads crisscrossed between two sheets of heavyweight oil-skin paper. They feel much like a rain slicker, and perform like one too. A little water will not affect a pretreated target face, whereas a plain paper one will disintegrate. Of course even the best equipment should not be left outdoors for prolonged periods of time. See Chapter 8, "Equipment Maintenance," for tips on caring for target equipment.

Target Stands

In regulation target archery, the mat is then placed on an easel so that the center of the target face is elevated 4 ft., 3 in. above the ground. Easels, also known as "target stands," may be of wood or metal, but wood is the traditional material. In the days when all arrows were made of wood, they would easily crack if they hit an extremely hard or unyielding surface, hence the wooden easel. Now that we have fiberglass and aluminum arrows, many archery clubs and schools are buying tubular metal easels. Their biggest advantage over wood is that they are weather-resistant, thereby significantly reducing maintenance. Wood has a tendency to rot, especially around the legs, and is constantly in need of reinforcement and repainting. Another advantage of metal easels is that they are lighter in weight, making them much easier to move around the archery range or to bring in for winter storage. If you are buying one for personal use and you will have to take care of it yourself, a metal easel may be more cost effective.

Wind Flags

To help you judge wind direction, a flag known as a "wind flag" may be placed on top of or behind your target stand. The flag should be of a bright color so that you can easily see and determine its movement. At longer distances, wind will affect arrow flight considerably, especially with lighter-weight tackle. Even at big-time tournaments, wind flags are used, so feel free to get one and install it on your target stand. If you're going to make it a permanent installation, a plastic flag will be more weather resistant than cloth.

4

CLOTHING & ACCESSORIES

If you decide to become involved with competitive archery, various sanctioning bodies have specific rules as to what is allowed at a particular event. These rules include everything from basic tackle to clothing and accessories. In this chapter, we'll examine some optional accessories you may wish to acquire, but be sure to check the rules for your intended event—be it organized competition or recreational shooting—to make sure your attire and equipment meet all requirements.

Casual Wear

One of the great benefits of archery is that you don't need to lay in an entire new wardrobe to get started shooting and having fun. Yes, competitive archery has apparel requirements (which we'll discuss later), but you don't need to buy new clothes to start. You will want to wear study, comfortable athletic shoes.

Your feet are your anchor, so sturdy shoes worn with sweat-absorbing socks are essential. Next you will need a comfortable pair of shorts or long trousers. On the top half, a T-shirt or polo shirt is a good choice. They allow more freedom of movement and are less structured than a fitted shirt or blouse. Finally, if you're shooting out-of-doors, you may wish to wear a cap to keep the sun off your head and out of your eyes.

One final note, archers of all ages should remember to secure long hair in an elastic band or by some other means. Long hair can get tangled in the bowstring. Not only would this cause an errant shot, it would hurt terribly when the bowstring shot forward, pulling your hair along with it.

Formal Attire

When young archers in the Junior Olympic Archery Development (JOAD) program compete at a sanctioned event, they are to wear white attire. They may wear an appropriate emblem representing their club on their shirt, and the emblem may be of any size or color. JOAD archers may not, however, wear advertising logos of any company unless there is a sponsorship agreement between the NAA and the company. There is a reason for wearing white clothing. It is not simply a matter of esthetics, white reflects sunlight, heat and radiation—all

Photo courtesy of NAA

This young archer is appropriately attired in a white shirt with her JOAD club emblem. Her hair is neatly tied back to keep it out of her way.

environmental factors that could make a long day out-of-doors very uncomfortable if not properly attired. The white clothing is required for your comfort and well-being.

The "clothing shield" can be worn anytime, either for recreational shooting or at an officially sanctioned competition. The clothing shield fits over the shoulder of the bow arm, covers the upper half of the chest, and is secured by an elastic strap around the back. The purpose of the shield is to keep your shirt from getting tangled in the bowstring.

Photo courtesy of NAA

Note the clothing shield worn over the shoulder of the bow
arm. It prevents clothing from getting tangled in the
bowstring.

Accessories

Although it is not necessary to have all the options
and accessories just to get started, the more you
know about archery equipment, the better you will
understand the sport. Furthermore, it's easier to
improve your game when you know which
accessories are available to help correct particular
problems. Here is a partial list of archery accessories,
namely the basic pieces familiar to most archers. By
no means is this list all-inclusive, but these items
will address most situations. Increase your collection
of accessories as you see fit, but do not feel that you

Photo courtesy of Lloyd Brown

Plastic armguard with two elastic bands protects the inner arm on the bow hand.

have to buy everything the first day. Concentrate on learning the basics and having fun.

Armguard—An armguard protects your bow arm from getting zapped by the bowstring. A good armguard must have two or more elastic straps with either hooks and eyes or velcro fastenings. It should be large enough to protect your arm, yet fit snugly enough to stay in place without restricting circulation or hindering your movements. Some archers prefer the new plastic armguards, but if you prefer the traditional leather, buy one with metal stays sewn inside to keep it stiff. Beginning archers may find it more comfortable to use the full-length style which reaches from the base of the wrist to the inner elbow.

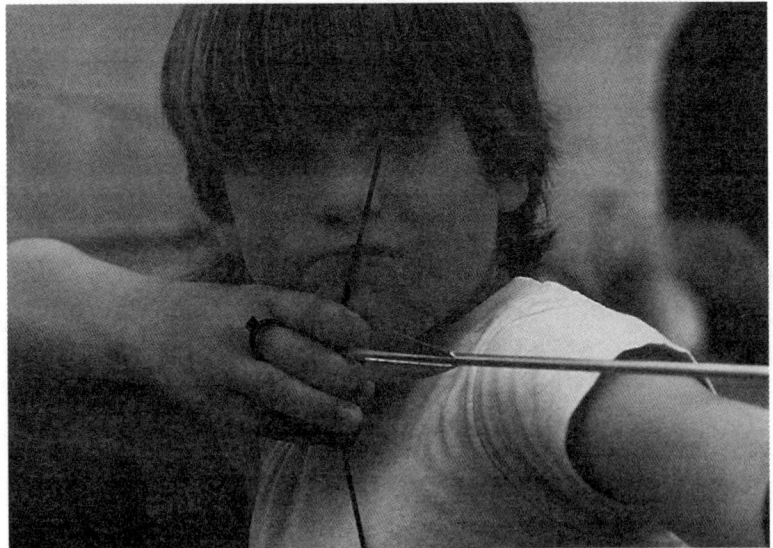

Photo courtesy of NAA

The finger tab is attached to the middle finger of the shooting hand by a loop or hole in the base of the tab.

Bow Tip Protectors—Think of them as booties for the ends of your bow. Tip protectors help keep the delicate ends of a bow from being damaged and the protector on the lower limb keeps the bowsting from getting away when the bow is unstrung. Remove tip protectors before shooting.

Clicker—A clicker is a device, made of springy metal, attached to the bow. You place the arrow under the clicker. When the arrow has been pulled to full draw, the tip of the arrow will slide past the clicker and the device will snap back against the bow, making a "click" sound as it does so. This sound tells the archer that he or she has reached full draw. An archery tackle shop can add a clicker to your bow at a later date. It is not essential that you purchase both at the same time.

Finger Tab—A finger tab is a thin piece of lightly padded leather or rubber, secured to the middle finger of your shooting hand by means of a loop or hole in the base of the tab. It allows for a smooth release and prevents the bowstring from "cutting" into your skin.

Glove—The three-finger shooting glove performs the same functions as does the finger tab, but offers more complete coverage. It attaches around the wrist, has elastic backing up to the fingers, and three finger caps into which you place your first, middle, and third fingers. As it tends to be a bit more stable, beginners may find the glove easier to work with when they are first learning to shoot. The choice of finger tab or shooting glove is largely a matter of personal choice. If possible, try both items before buying one, then select the style that works best for you.

Photo courtesy of NAA

This type of sight, mounted just above the grip, can be adjusted for various distances.

Quiver—Although one traditionally thinks of a quiver as being worn across the back, attached by a strap around the chest, today's archers are more apt to use the belt quiver. It does not interfere with shooting and it is easier to retrieve arrows from the belt quiver. There are many styles available. Let your personal taste and your budget be your guide.

Photo courtesy of NAA

A telescope mounted on a tripod helps this young archer check his target position.

Release Aid—A release aid is hooked onto the bowstring at the nocking point and the archer draws the release aid instead of the bowstring itself. When using a release aid, the fingers are turned outward, or the hand can be held in a horizontal position with the fingers pointing toward the ground. When the archer is satisfied that his aim is accurate and the arrow is at full draw, the release aid is opened, thereby freeing the bow to shoot the arrow. The purpose of a release aid is that it prevents the drawing fingers from imparting a twist to the string.

Scope—Whether you use a telescope mounted on a tripod or a pair of binoculars, a scope of some type will help you spot your target position. Scopes are popular with tournament archers and they use this information to make adjustments in their aim. If you are just learning to shoot, you will probably be close enough to your target to see with the naked eye. Moreover, the minuscule adjustments made by competitive archers are usually unnecessary for recreational shooting.

Sight—A sight is a device attached to the bow above the grip. Its purpose is to help the archer find true vertical and, thereby, improve his or her aim. Most sights have one or more aiming pins, adjustable both horizontally and vertically. The most sophisticated sights have bubble levels to tell the archer when the bow is exactly on the vertical. If you are interested in entering an archery competition, however, make sure you know the rules governing that particular event. Some sights may be prohibited in certain classifications.

Slings—There are a number of different types of slings, but all serve to keep the archer from accidentally dropping the bow, especially for those advanced archers using an open-handed grip. The finger sling attaches around the index finger and thumb of the bow hand. After the release and as a phase of the follow through, the upper bow arm rocks forward. The finger sling prevents the bow from falling to the ground. The basic wrist sling is a leather strap attached to the grip of the bow, and looped around the archer's wrist, hence the name wrist sling. It too prevents the bow from falling.

Photo courtesey of NAA

This bow is fitted with a stabilizer below the handgrip. It looks awkward but actually prevents movement and vibration.

Stabilizer—A stabilizer is a rod, or number of rods, attached to the bow. These rods can extend front, backward, sideways, or in all three directions. At first glance, the rods give the bow somewhat of a "science fiction" look, but they are highly effective and of great benefit, especially to target archers.

Their purpose is to absorb vibration in the bow when it is shot, thereby reducing torque and other excess movements, and giving the bow greater stability.

𝍐5

FITNESS & NUTRITION

Selecting your equipment and accessories is only the beginning. For best results, before you began shooting, get your "archery muscles" toned and strengthened. The physical and mental demands of archery competition are extensive, but even recreational archers will have a better time, *i.e.*, shoot more accurately and be less tired, if they undergo a basic conditioning program prior to shooting.

Archery is predominately an upper-body sport, meaning that the muscles of the hands, arms, neck, back and abdominals are those taking the most stress. For this reason archery is an excellent sport for physically-challenged athletes who have upper body dexterity, but may be unable to participate in running or other lower-body-oriented sports. In fact, some of the highest scores recorded in indoor archery are routinely posted by archers shooting from their wheelchairs.

The Purpose of Conditioning

The physical demands of a tournament are determined by (1) the type of event including time,

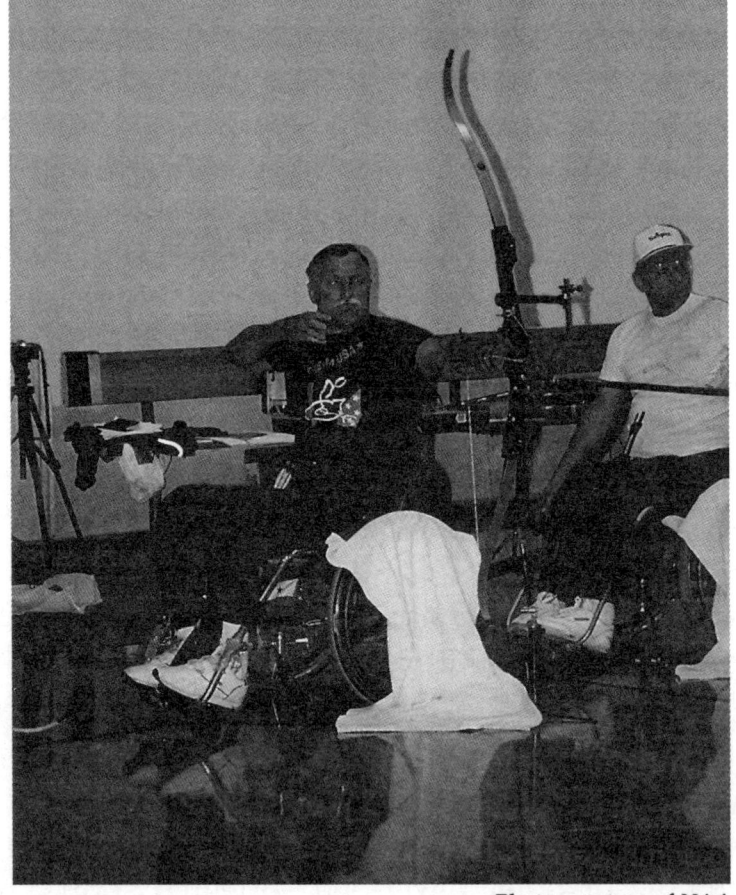

Photo courtesy of NAA

Archery is an excellent sport for physically-challenged athletes. High scores are routinely posted by wheelchair-bound archers.

length, distance to cover, and number of arrows; (2) the size of the individual; (3) bow poundage and weight; (4) environmental conditions such as temperature and humidity; and (5) the overall fitness level of the archer. These same conditions can be applied to recreational archery, and you will have a more enjoyable experience if you are fit for the task. Of course the benefits you will derive from any training program are relative to how you train. For example, strength training certainly makes you stronger, but it does little to increase flexibility, so you should plan to include a variety of exercises into your overall program. To select a program, first determine your primary goals and objectives. Obviously you would have to train harder to be competitive in international tournaments than you would to simply shoot a few arrows in the backyard, but the point is you want to find a general conditioning program that's right for you.

Begin by evaluating you present state of fitness. Only by knowing where you are can you understand where you need to go. The basic components of physical fitness for archery are (1) muscular strength; (2) muscular endurance; (3) flexibility; (4) body composition; and (5) cardiovascular fitness. Each of these components are related to both overall health and archery performance. Here's how they work:

- Muscular strength and endurance are important for the repeated muscular contractions needed while shooting.

- Flexibility is needed in the upper body (shoulders, arms, fingers, back, neck and abdominals).

- Body composition relates to your overall health and effects your ability to perform.

- Cardiovascular fitness is important to help you meet the demands of an archery tournament or to hike the hills and dales on a field archery shoot.

Muscle Imbalance

It is important to condition both sides of your body; and in archery, because we think of always drawing the bowstring on the same side of our body, that fact can get overlooked. As you work through your exercises, be sure to work both sides of your body equally. Another thing you can do is to practice drawing the bowstring with your opposite hand. It will feel awkward at first, but keep practicing. It will get easier and you will be conditioning your left and right sides in equal amounts.

Strength Exercises

Drawing A Bow—This exercise is similar to shooting, only without the arrows. Draw, stretch and contract muscles. Hold each draw for 6 seconds; relax and gently return bowstring to its resting position. Work both sides of your body, alternating arms.

Sit Ups—Lie on the ground with knees slightly bent and feet flat on the ground. If you need extra support, put a rolled towel under the small of your back. Put your hands behind your head, elbows flat to the ground. Raise up just enough that your head and shoulders come off the ground. While rising, elbows swing inward and point toward your knees. Return to the starting position and repeat.

Sit Ups

Illustrations in this chapter courtesty of NAA

Flying Eagle—You may wish to purchase a set of free weights so you can increase the amount of weight as you progress. But a can of soup, held in each hand, is an easy (and effective) way to get started. Stand in an open area, well away from any walls, or sit on the

Flying Eagle

edge of a bench or a chair without arms. Hold your arms at your sides, then raise them out like wings. Hold for a count of 5, slowly return to the starting position. Repeat.

There are other strengthening exercises of course, but most require access to some type of resistance-training equipment, the type of machines found in a gym. If you are interested in serious strength training, joining a gym may be your best bet. Tell the trainer that you are an archer, and let him or her develop an exercise program for you that will enhance your shooting.

Flexibility Exercises

The following are some general stretching exercises you can do at home. None require additional equipment. Be sure to wear comfortable, lightweight clothing and well-padded athletic shoes with socks. The clothing will give you the most flexibility and good shoes will protect your bones and joints from concussion.

Upper Body Stretches

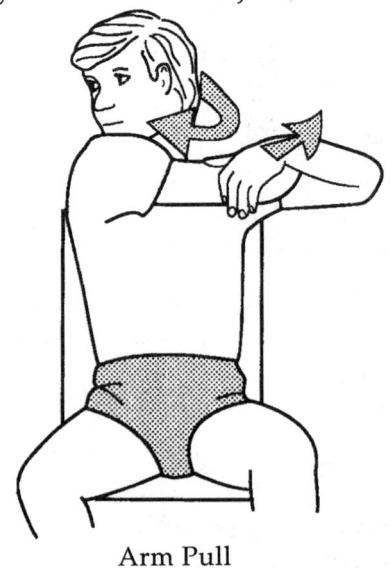

Arm Pull—Pull your left arm across your chest and rotate your head over your left shoulder. Hold for a count of 5. Now stretch your right arm and look over your right shoulder. Alternating arms, repeat 3 times.

Arm Pull

Twist and Shout—Stand a few inches out from a wall. Place both feet facing forward and slightly bend the knees. Now, keeping your knees forward as best you can, twist your upper torso to the left

Twist and Shout

and place both palms flat on the wall. Now twist to the right and place both palms flat on the wall. This is an excellent warm-up exercise that stretches both sides of your body.

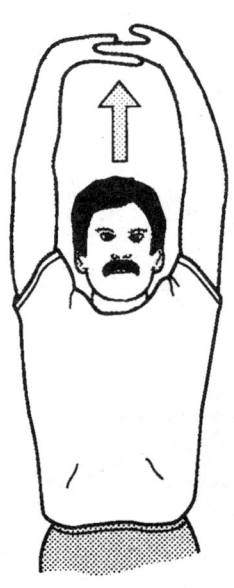

Shoulder Stretch—Raise both arms over your head and interlock your fingers. Reach as high as you can, keeping your palms turned toward the ceiling. Hold for a count of 10. Stretches both sides of your trunk and wrists.

Shoulder Stretch

Behind Your Back—
Stand up. In this
exercise you will try
to grasp your hands
behind you back.
Reach one arm over
your shoulder and
behind your back,
and the other arm
reach under your
shoulder and behind
your back. Repeat by
alternating   arm
positions. Stretches
the shoulder and
neck area.

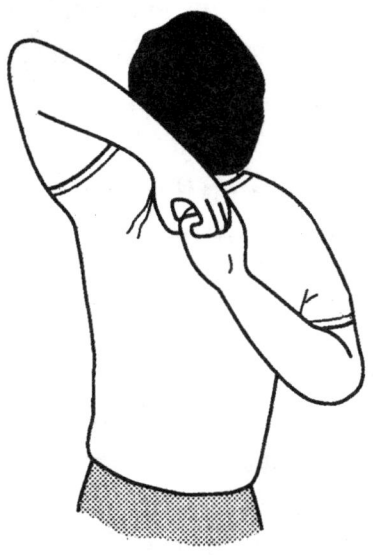

Behind Your Back

Lower Body Stretches
Groin Stretch—Sit on
the floor, open your
knees and bring your
heels toward you.
Gently hold your
thighs down with
your arms. Do not
bounce. Stretches the
inner thigh muscles.

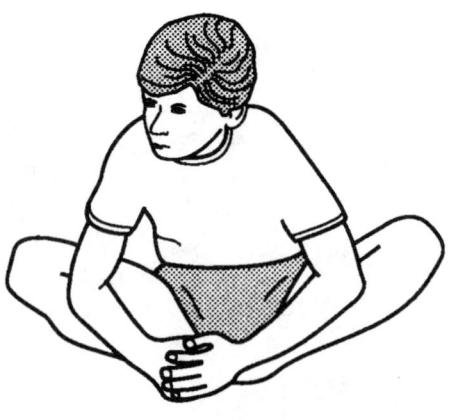

Groin Stretch

Hip Stretch—Lie on the ground and bring the knee toward the chest, other leg extended. This stretches the hamstring muscles. Repeat other leg.

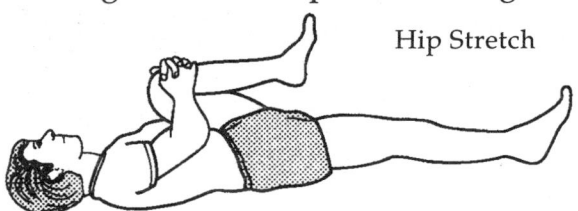

Hip Stretch

Bunny Hop—Balance against a wall. Stand on one leg and bend the other back. Grab your toes with your free hand and gently pull your leg up behind you. Don't pull too far. This stretches the big muscle in front of the thigh. Hold for a count of 5 and do the other leg.

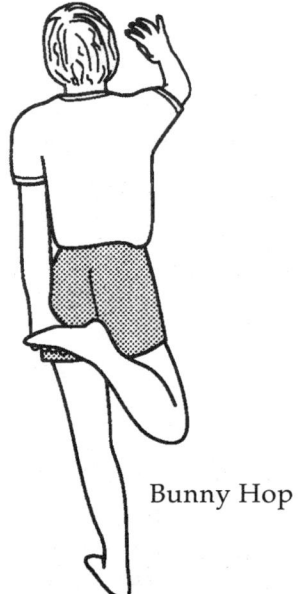

Bunny Hop

Nutrition

Your diet is an important part of your overall physical fitness. Basically, food is broken down into three forms: carbohydrates, fats and protein. All are vital for good health, but athletes most often focus complex carbohydrates found in such foods as potatoes, bread, pasta, lentils, vegetables and nuts. In addition to the necessary starch found in these foods, they also provide all the vitamins and minerals necessary to metabolize (break down) the carbohydrates. The assimilation process is essential if the body is to utilize the nutrients found in the foods. Without it, the nutrients pass right through the body, giving little or no benefit.

Simple carbohydrates, found in confectionery, processed foods and soft drinks, provide quick energy, but offer no lasting benefits. Consumption of these foods and drinks should be kept to a minimum.

Few people in the western world need to fear that they are not getting enough fat in their diet. On the whole, we should reduce the amount of fat we ingest, not look around for more. Some fat, of course, is essential for good health, but the amount of fat in the average diet is already excessive. Fat is beneficial in that it ultimately serves as a long-range source of energy, but your primary source of fuel should be carbohydrates, not fat.

Protein is the athlete's friend. Among its many duties, protein builds and repairs muscle tissue, and every athlete wants and needs strong, healthy muscles. The best sources of protein are white meats, fish, beans, legumes, nuts and goat's milk.

It's important to fuel your body before you embark in a long, tournament or recreational field event, but avoid excess fat and any foods difficult to digest. After all, the purpose of your meal is to give you energy, not a belly ache. If you have additional questions about good food choices for archers, consult your doctor. You may also find helpful information by contacting the sports medicine department of various universities.

Archery
Fundamentals

By this time you have selected your tackle and accessories, located a spot suitable for archery and safe from passersby, and set up the equipment you'll need such as scopes, targets and wind flags. Of course, if you are shooting with a club or at an official archery range, the targets and flags will already be in place.

Stringing The Bow

Before you can shoot, you must attach the bowstring. This process is known as "stringing the bow." It is not complicated once you do it a few times, but in the interest of protecting yourself and your bow, ask an experienced archer or tackle shop staffer to show you how. There are many devices for stringing a bow, some more elaborate and expensive than others.

All have the same goal, however, to secure the bowstring to the bow, making it ready for shooting.

Some bow stringers can be permanently attached to the wall and these are a good choice for archery clubs and groups with a regular clubhouse. If you are shooting at home, you may prefer a simple cord stringer which can be rolled up and tossed into your gear bag once you are finished.

Regardless of which procedure you use, the string's bottom loop must be securely seated in the bottom notches before bending the bow. The larger loop of the bowstring is always placed around the upper limb with the smaller fitting into the notches of the lower limb. The stringing procedure will place the upper loop in the notches of the upper limb. All stringers come with directions for their use, and experienced archers will always be glad to help you if you need assistance.

Now that your bow is strung, you have loaded your arrows into your quiver, and arrived at the shooting line, it's time to begin. Of course archery technique, as in all sports, is a complicated business. The following is by no means a complete description of archery technique. This is just a quick-reference check list, as recommended by the NAA, to help you pinpoint the basics. For more thorough training, join a sanctioned archery club or ask an experienced archer for assistance.

Stance

Stand perpendicular to your target, feet straddling the shooting line and shoulder-width apart. Balance your body weight over the balls of your feet. Stand tall and keep you spine straight, but not ramrod stiff—you need your body to absorb the recoil and you can't do this properly if you are overly stiff. Place your back foot (that is the foot behind the shooting line) parallel with the line, now angle your forward foot slightly toward the target. Keep your knees gently relaxed.

Nock

Nocking the arrow specifically means to place the arrow nock onto the bowstring, but in the broader sense it means to perform all the steps associated with getting the arrow ready to shoot. Determine that the index feather points away from the bow. Lay the arrow on the arrowrest and snap the nock onto the bowstring under the nocking point on the string. (If you are using a clicker, you should make sure the arrow is under the clicker as you place it on the arrowrest.)

Set

Grasp the bow exactly the same way every time. This not only produces good work habits, it helps ensure consistent draw and aids in accuracy. Arrange the bow into the nook, *i.e.*, meaty part between the thumb and index finger, of your bow hand. Develop a comfortable, but not overly-tight, grip. Once your bow hand is set, take the string in the first joint of the first three fingers of the shooting hand. If you are using a three-finger shooting glove or finger tab, make sure your accessories fit properly and are in good working order. You may either enclose the arrow between the first and second fingers, or place all three fingers under the arrow.

Pre-Draw

Raise the bow toward your target. Lock your bow arm into position and turn your elbow out. (If you forgot to put on your armguard stop and do it now, then repeat the steps starting with the stance. Do not fire an arrow without your armguard in place.)

Draw

With the shoulder of your bow arm pushing and the shoulder of your drawing arm pulling, draw the bowstring until it touches your nose and lips. Except in the case of an emergency, never stop your drawing motion once you have begun. To do so produces an erratic, uneven flight and takes the power out of the release. Your elbow should stop behind and slightly above (never below) your shoulder.

Anchor

The anchor is the final stage of the draw and the two should flow as one motion. Specifically, the anchor refers to resting your drawing hand against your face, prior to the aim and release. You may choose to

Photo courtesy of NAA

Draw the string until it touches the side of your nose and the center of your lips. This archer is using an under-the-chin anchor.

Photo courtesy of NAA

This archer is using a beside-the-cheek anchor. The elbow
of the bow hand is properly turned out and the elbow of
the drawing hand is correctly above the shoulder.

anchor either under your chin or beside your cheek.
Either is acceptable and you should experiment
with both anchors to find which works best for you.

Aim

At this stage, your concentration will shift to your
bowsight and target. Do not be overly concerned if
the bullseye seems to "swim" in and out of your
bowsight. By the time the arrow reaches its target it
will have compensated for any irregularity in sight
alignment.

Release

As the back muscles continue to tighten at the moment of release, the drawing hand completely relaxes and the string escapes from the hand. Let the tension in your back muscles pull your drawing hand straight back along your neck. Congratulations, your arrow is launched.

Follow through

As soon as the arrow leaves the bow, continue pulling your drawing hand back along the base of your neck. Allow the bow to gently rock forward in your bow hand. A bow sling will keep it from falling to the ground. Follow through is an important part of shooting; don't neglect this element of your overall technique.

As mentioned earlier, there are many steps to perfecting your shooting technique. The aforementioned are simply an outline of the basics. If you are working alone, however, these basics will get you off to a good start. If you have the benefit of an instructor, you will progress that much quicker. If you are interested in taking lessons, some YMCA and YWCA chapters offer archery classes, or contact the NAA for information about a club in your area. If there is no club, perhaps you can be the person to start one.

7

Safety & First Aid

Among archery's many benefits is that it is a sport remarkably free from accident or injury. This, of course, simply adds to archery's attraction and enables people of all ages and physical condition to join the fun. Even with archery's excellent safety record, however, athletes in every sport realize that a mishap can happen to anyone at any time. No matter where you are shooting, it's a good idea simply to have a first aid kit on hand and to be aware of a few steps that can be taken in an emergency. This information may be especially interesting to those engaged in field archery where the hazards of the trail can sometimes get you, even under the best of circumstances. No doubt more people have suffered bug bites and heat stroke than any mishap with archery tackle, per se.

The First Aid Kit
It's a good idea to keep a basic first aid kit on hand at all times. Many pharmacies and sporting goods

stores carry well-stocked first aid kits, but if you want to put one together yourself, the following items should be included:

- Adhesive bandages of various sizes
- Ammonia caps (for dizziness)
- Antiseptic soap (for washing a wounded area)
- Antiseptic solution (for bug bites, minor scrapes)
- Aspirin
- Blanket (warmth reduces chance of shock)
- Cold packs
- Elastic bandages (various sizes)
- Eyewash solution
- Gauze pads (various sizes)
- Non-stick gauze pads (for covering wounds)
- Scissors
- Tissues and pre-moistened towelettes
- Tweezers (for splinters)
- Small utility knife

The phone number of the nearest ambulance service should be taped to the inside of the first aid kit. If you shoot as a club or group, all archers should know where the first aid kit is stored and where it will be kept at all events. The best first aid kit in the world does you no good if you can't find it when you need it. When shooting at an unfamiliar location, make sure someone in your group knows the location of the closest telephone; and always keep a quarter or two in the kit so you won't have to run in circles, hunting for change in an emergency.

Vision & Corrective Lenses

Your vision, just like the strength in your arms and legs, is an important part of your overall performance, and the demands on your visual system during sporting activities are rigorous. To shoot your best, you must be able to sight your target, and this takes a variety of vision skills. If your natural vision inhibits your performance, ask your doctor about corrective lenses.

Today's eye care practitioners utilize a wide variety of lens materials. One such development is the new impact-resistant lens now available for use in prescription glasses. These lenses are cosmetically excellent, reasonable in cost, light weight, and will not shatter if broken. Some archers find that glasses interfere with their draw, but others say they have no problem wearing glasses at all. It is an individual decision, and you may want to try shooting with and without glasses to see which works best for you.

Another option is contact lenses. Available in hard and soft lens materials, contacts offer many excellent advantages to the athlete. For best results, tell your doctor about the type of sports you play. That information will be helpful to the doctor in selecting the best lenses for you. If you wear contact lenses, take your cleaning and wetting solutions with you to all archery events, and notify your coach that you are wearing contacts.

Getting a foreign object in the eye is the most common eye problem associated with outdoor sports. Fortunately, these foreign objects are usually in the form of minor irritants such as dust, dirt, or sand. Goggles will help protect your eyes, and many archers find that the wraparound-type does not hinder their draw. There are many styles to chose from—select one that fits securely and provides the best vision.

Care of the Eyes

More serious contusions, such as a blow to the head, may produce bleeding in or under the skin, causing a "black eye." An ice pack will reduce swelling until a doctor can evaluate the injury.

Fortunately, the eye has a number of natural protective mechanisms. It is recessed in a bony socket, the quick-blinking reflexes of the eyelids and eyelashes deflect most foreign particles, and natural tears wash away most minor irritants. If you *do* get something in your eye, follow these simple guidelines:

- Do not rub your eye or use a dirty cloth or finger to remove the obstruction.

- Irritants can often be eliminated by looking down and pulling the eyelid forward and down. Make sure your hands are clean.

- If you see a particle floating on your eye, gently remove it with a clean, sterile cloth or apply an eye wash to flush the obstruction.

Whatever your recreational activity, your vision plays a vital role in helping you enjoy the sport and perform at peak efficiency. Your eyes deserve the best of care.

Wrist, Hand & Finger Injuries

Injuries to the wrists, hands and fingers are most often related to fatigue. To reduce the possibility of wrist, hand and finger injuries, follow these simple guidelines:

- Prior to shooting, remove all cosmetic jewelry. If you wear a medical alert bracelet, continue to wear it, but make sure it is snug enough not to catch on your equipment or get tangled in the bowstring.

- Avoid holding the bow with your fingers straight out. Keep you finger tips and knuckles curled back toward your palms, and keep your thumb resting along the side of your index finger.

- Avoid putting a "death grip" on your bow. Hold your bow firmly, but allow some flex into your arm, back, and shoulder muscles. This will help reduce stress and fatigue from settling in your hands, thereby reducing your chances of wrist and hand injuries.

- Tabs or finger gloves are a good way to protect your shooting hand, and if the weather is especially cold, a regular glove on your bow hand will keep it warm, making shooting more comfortable. Some archers use a glove on sunny days to reduce the chance of sunburn. This is a personal choice, and you should try shooting with and without gloves to see which works best for you.

Transporting Tips

To be on the safe side, anyone who has suffered an upper extremity injury should be evaluated by a doctor. To safely transport a person with an arm, wrist, hand or finger injury, follow these steps:

- A finger with mild swelling can be gently taped to an adjacent finger.

- An elastic bandage may be gently wrapped around an injured wrist to give the wrist support. Do not wrap heavily and do not pull the bandage tight.

- If possible, place a pillow in the injured person's lap and allow him or her to rest the injured hand on the pillow. Do not bunch the pillow around the injury. To do so may cause pressure points.

Ice & Heat Treatments

If an injury occurs, elevate the injured extremity and apply an ice pack. Use ice instead of heat because cold reduces both swelling and pain. Leave the ice pack on until it becomes uncomfortable for the

Photo courtesy of Easton

To ensure safety, routinely check mats and target stands. Worn straw should be replaced and weakened legs repaired.

person—the time varies with each individual. Allow the injured person to rest quietly for 15 minutes, then reapply the ice pack. Repeat this procedure until any swelling abates or, in more serious cases, until professional medical help can arrive.

In most cases, after two or three days or when the swelling has stopped, heat can be applied in the form of warm-water soaks. Fifteen minutes of warm soaking, along with a gradual return to motion, will speed the healing process right along. If you are having pain, check with a physician before

Photo courtesy of NAA

Checking your score is half the fun, but target area can get very crowded. Take care not to hit anyone when pulling arrows.

undertaking any type of do-it-yourself treatment. It may also be a good idea to have a physician examine your injury before you return to archery.

Guidelines for Reducing Injuries

Although no amount of planning and preparation can guarantee that no one at a field or target range will ever be injured, there are many things that can be done to reduce the possibilities of a mishap.

- Go over your arrow nocks occasionally, using a magnifying glass if possible. Locate any cracks in the plastic, and replace damaged nocks right away.

- Fiberglass and aluminum shafts are stronger that wood, but they too must be checked for straightness. If a particular arrow continually produces erratic flight, it may be damaged inside the shaft, even if it appears to be okay on the outside. Ask an experienced archer to check it for you.

- Wood arrows require special attention. Inspect wood shafts for cracks and splinters. If you detect a crack, break the arrow in half and discard it. Cracked arrows will only ruin your shooting (not to mention your score). Get rid of damaged arrows and replace them as needed. Sometimes bent arrows can be steamed back into place, but this is a job for experienced hands. Report any bent arrows to your club leader, or take them to an authorized archery tackle shop. The staff there may be able to fix them for you or offer other sound advice.

- For arrows, proper storage is the key to longevity. Never bunch arrows together, this damages their fletching. If possible, store them in their original box or on an arrow rack. Never pile anything on top of arrows as the weight will cause them to bend.

- Remember, *your* objective is to avoid an accident, let the authorities handle any complaints.
- Watch where you are walking. Stray arrows often get lodged in the ground, especially around the target area. Keep an eye out for fletching and avoid stepping on a fallen arrow.

8

EQUIPMENT MAINTENANCE

Archery equipment will last longer and function more effectively when it is properly maintained. It is neither difficult nor time consuming to maintain the tackle, and you will probably find that taking care of your equipment is almost as much fun as shooting. If you belong to a JOAD club, organize a maintenance day as a club project. A good time for such an endeavor would be just before winter when targets must be put up for the year, or in the spring when its time to ready the equipment for another season. Ask your instructor or club leader when it would be most convenient to have a work party, then call in the troops. Maintenance work always seems to go quicker when shared with fellow archers.

Bows & Strings

Caring for a bow and strings is relatively simple. Some of these points should be employed on a daily basis, while others refer to occasional or one-time maintenance.

- Attach the bow sight to the bow with screws, not tape. The adhesive will become sticky in hot weather, picking up dust and debris and making your hand sticky as well. Also, tape has been known to damage the finish on some bows.

- Never lay a bow on the ground. It can be accidentally stepped on, and severely damaged as a result. Moreover, dropping a bow on the ground knocks it out of alignment and out of tune. Treat all bows carefully, yours and everyone else's.

- Although finishes are waterproof, it is best to dry the bow if it gets wet. Use a soft, absorbent material such as terrycloth. An old hand towel is a good thing to keep in your locker or pack. It provides the softness and absorbency for taking care of tackle and can be easily washed itself when necessary.

- Carefully wipe and dry all metal parts, paying particular attention to your sight and clicker. Direct rain is not the only culprit, even a damp, foggy day, can produce enough moisture to cause trouble if tackle is not wiped dry before being put away. Simply wipe your gear down after every shoot and you won't have a problem.

- Bow wax, applied as needed, will help preserve the life of your bow.

  If you do not have bow wax, a gentle, non-abrasive furniture wax can be used instead.

- Recurve bows should be unstrung when not in use, and all bows should be transported in bow cases and stored on bow racks. Never store a bow by standing it on end. Left this way for any length of time, the stress on the lower limb produced by the weight of the bow may cause the limb to warp or twist.

- Compound bows need to have their pulleys lubricated from time to time. For best results, follow manufacturer's recommendations regarding frequency and type of lubricant.

- Never leave a bow in a hot, airtight place such as a car or trunk. The heat may soften the glue of the laminations and the weight of the handle riser may cause the limbs to become twisted.

- Remove any dirt or sand that has collected in the string nocks on the bow limbs. Grit of any kind is abrasive to the bowstring and may cause it to fray. Likewise, look for fraying or other signs of weakness in the strands of the bowstring. Wax bowstrings occasionally, including your spares. If you're not sure how to do this, consult a reputable tackle shop and ask their advice. They will always be glad to help you.

Arrows

With the invention of fiberglass and aluminum shafts, archers now have a wider variety of materials to choose from. Maintenance, however, is basically the same, regardless of construction, and all arrows will perform better when cared for properly.

- Feathers on arrows should be kept dry. If the fletching becomes wet, separating the arrows until they are dry will allow the feathers to expand and regain their original shape. If the feathers are matted down, they can be steamed to return them to their original shape. Ask your club leader to help you if feathers need to be steamed. Check plastic vanes for debris, wipe them clean, and store so that vanes are not compromised in any way.

- Always use the proper method of pulling arrows from targets. Grasp the arrow close to where it entered the target and place your other hand flat against the target— ideally so that the arrow sticks out between you thumb and index finger. Push against the target with the one hand, and with the other pull the arrow straight back. Never rock an arrow back and forth, that does nothing but bend the arrow and ruin the target. If your arrowhead is stuck, grasp it with a pair of pliers or use a knife to dig the arrowhead from the wood. (This is one reason why you carry a utility knife in your first aid kit.)

- Go over your arrow nocks occasionally, using a magnifying glass if possible. Locate any cracks in the plastic, and replace damaged nocks right away.

- Fiberglass and aluminum shafts are stronger that wood, but they too must be checked for straightness. If a particular arrow continually produces erratic flight, it may be damaged inside the shaft, even if it appears to be okay on the outside. Ask an experienced archer to check it for you.

- Wood arrows require special attention. Inspect wood shafts for cracks and splinters. If you detect a crack, break the arrow in half and discard it. Cracked arrows will only ruin your shooting (not to mention your score). Get rid of damaged arrows and replace them as needed. Sometimes bent arrows can be steamed back into place, but this is a job for experienced hands. Report any bent arrows to your club leader, or take them to an authorized archery tackle shop. The staff there may be able to fix them for you or offer other sound advice.

- For arrows, proper storage is the key to longevity. Never bunch arrows together, this damages their fletching. If possible, store them in their original box or on an arrow rack. Never pile anything on top of arrows as the weight will cause them to bend.

Targets

Whether you use professionally-constructed mats or a simple bale of straw, your target will last longer with good care. If you are shooting at home or in any other location where the mat or straw bale remains in place year round, construct a protective roof over the sight. If that's not possible, keep the target covered with heavy plastic and a waterproof tarp. If you use a straw bale, place bricks or logs under the bale. Keeping it up off damp ground will prolong its usefulness.

- Target faces should always be removed before mats are stored away for the winter. Even during the archery season if you suspect inclement weather, you may wish to retrieve the target face and keep it in a dry location.

- Plain paper targets should be glued to a piece of cardboard. Without the reinforcement, they soon will be torn to shreds—if not by arrows, then by the wind and sun. Masking tape applied to the back of a hole or tear will also reinforce the area.

- If target stands are left outdoors on a large grassy area watered by automatic irrigation, ask the groundskeeper to turn the sprinkler heads so that they avoid shooting the targets as much as possible. Sometimes this simply isn't possible, but give it a go and see what, if anything, can be done to spare your equipment.

- New target mats come with instructions for their care, including moistening and tightening. Follow these procedures carefully. Never stack freshly-moistened mats against each other. This will increase the possibility of spontaneous combustion. Keep them separated where they can get maximum air flow.

- To prevent mildew and rot, never store mats on a damp floor.
- At least twice a year check target stands for wood rot. If a stand were to collapse on someone's hand or foot, the consequences could be severe. Repair weakened stands immediately and fill any damp holes with sand before repositioning the equipment. Dampness is a sign that water accumulates in that spot. Sand is more porous than dirt and will allow for better drainage around the target stand's legs.

Target mats require special storage space. They should not be stood on end, to do so makes them weaken and lose their shape. They should be stored flat, well up off the ground, on specially-built shelves, holding one mat per shelf. To allow maximum circulation, each shelf should be separated with four-by-six boards. Mats should be stored out of direct sunlight and away from dampness.

Accessories

Chances are if you are just starting out, you won't have need to acquire much in the way of tackle accessories. Your equipment dealer will probably be able to supply you with all the parts and pieces you need. You probably will, however, have personal items such as armguards and/or finger gloves, and these items need a little care too.

Photo courtesy of NAA

Accessories such as wristbands, armguards and finger tabs should be cleaned and checked daily. You don't want an elastic band to break loose in the middle of a shot!

- All leather goods should be dried with a terrycloth towel and small pieces such as tabs should be stored where they can be laid flat. Do not let them get curved out of shape. To do so will have a negative impact on their effectiveness, not to mention their comfort. Damp leather should be dried and given a rubdown with leather oil or saddle soap. If the archery tackle shop doesn't have these items, you can find them at a saddle shop.

- Pieces with elastic parts, such as armguards or bow slings, should be checked and elastic replaced as needed. After all, you don't want your accessories to fail you right in the middle of a big meet.

If you take a few minutes each day to properly examine and care for your tackle and equipment, you will find that your gear will remain in good shape, ready to serve you whenever you are ready to shoot.

9

GLOSSARY

Like all sports, archery has a lexicon of its own. Being familiar with the language of archery will help you understand the sport and make you a better archer. Furthermore, using official terms to phrase a question or explain a situation will facilitate your communication with fellow archers, tackle store dealers, instructors, and officials.

Anchor—The position of the drawing hand at full draw. At high anchor the drawing hand touches the cheek. At low anchor the drawing hand is placed under the jaw bone.

Armguard—A piece of stiff material used to protect the bow arm from the bow string upon release. An armguard is usually made of leather and is worn on the inside of the forearm holding the bow.

Arrow Point—The metal tip of an arrow.

Arrowrest—A horizontal projection on the bow upon which the arrow lies. This device keeps the arrow on the bow and in shooting position.

Back—The outer surface or backside of a bow; the side facing the target.

Barebow—A conventional bow with no sights, stabilizers or draw checks.

Belly—The inner surface or inside of a bow; the side facing the bow string. Also called the *Face.*

Bolts—The short arrows used in a crossbow. Also called *Quarrels.*

Bow—A device made of flexible material with a string connecting the two ends. The string, when drawn and released, propels an arrow.

Bow Arm—The arm or hand which holds the bow.

Bow Notches—Grooves at either end of a bow that keep the bow string secured.

Bow Rack—A rack to hold archery bows when they are not in use. A bow rack makes a safe storage place and protects bows from damage.

Bow Sight—A mechanical device placed on a bow which the archer uses for aiming at the target. Not allowed in some types of archery competition.

Bow Sling—A strap fastened to either the bow or the archer's bow hand that keeps the bow from falling after the release. It is especially useful if the archer shoots with a relaxed bow hand.

Bowstringer—A device used to safely and effectively string a bow.

Brace Height—The distance between the braced bowstring and the handle of the bow. Also called the *String Height.*

Butt—Any backstop to which a target face is attached.

Cast—The ability of the bow to propel an arrow a given distance.

Centershot—The cutout section in the bow's upper limb just above the grip. In a full centershot bow, the arrow points straight ahead at full draw, instead of slightly off to one side as it does with a non-centershot bow.

Chest Protector—A piece of nylon mesh or leather worn across the chest to keep the bow string from catching on the archer's clothing.

Classification—Division of archers according to age and gender.

Clicker—A thin metal strip mounted on the bow which signals a draw of exactly the same length on each shot.

Clout Archery—A long-range archery competition in which the bullseye is laid on the ground, marked by a flag.

Cock Feather—The feather (or vane) at a right angle to the bowstring. The cock feather is a different color than the other feathers or vanes on the same arrow.

Composite Bow—A bow manufactured by combining different types of materials.

Compound Bow—A bow designed with pulleys. Unlike other bows, a compound bow is easiest to hold at full draw.

Creeping—A fault in shooting form in which the archer lets the arrow move, or creep, forward just before releasing the draw. This fault should be corrected as it weakens the shot, reducing both speed and distance.

Crest—Colored bands around the shafts of the arrows which aid in their identification. Especially helpful when more than one archer is shooting at the same target.

Crossbow—A bow mounted horizontally on a stock, similar to a gunstock. A crossbow shooter is always referred to as a *crossbowman*, not an archer.

Distance Markers—Markers placed on the field to indicate the distance from the shooting line to the target.

Double Scoring—A process by which two archers keep score at the target to eliminate errors.

Draw—*n*. The distance the bow string is pulled back. *v*. To pull the bow string back.

Draw Weight—The force, measured in pounds, necessary to pull the bow string a specific distance.

Easel—Target mat holder with wheels.

End—A predetermined number of arrows that are shot before going to the target to score and retrieve them.

Face—see *Belly*.

Feathers—Fletching made of common turkey feathers.

Field Archery—Competitive archery shot outdoors in a wooded area. Targets are of various sizes and archers shoot from different, standardized yardages.

Finger Sling—A strap that attaches to the thumb and index finger of the bow hand to support the bow when the string is released.

Fletching—The feathers, vanes or other devices attached to an arrow shaft which stabilize the flight of an arrow.

Flight Archery—Projecting an arrow to its greatest distance.

Follow through—Behavior of the body, especially the drawing hand and arm, after release of the string.

Freestyle—A classification of archery equipment where sights, stabilizers, draw checks and release aids are acceptable.

Freestyle Limited—A classification of archery equipment where sights, stabilizers and draw checks are acceptable, but release aids are not permitted.

Full Draw—The position of the archer when the bow string has been drawn and the draw hand is at the anchor point.

Glove—Three leather fingers worn on the drawing hand to protect the skin. The glove is held in place by a strap which fastens around the wrist.

Group—*n.* The pattern of arrows in a target face. *v.* To shoot arrows in a pattern.

Gunbarrel—A method of aiming used in bare bow shooting in which the nock end of the arrow is placed close to the eye and the archer sights down the arrow shaft.

Handicap—Points an archer legally receives to adjust his or her score in a tournament, thereby making the tournament more competitive.

Handle Riser—The thick portion of the bow from which the limbs extend. See *Limb*.

Kisser—A raised or thickened area on the bowstring that touches the archer's lips at full draw.

Laminated Bow—A bow made of several layers of different material glued together, usually two layers of fiberglass and a hardwood core.

Limb—The upper and lower parts of the bow above and below the handle riser. Energy is thus stored in the limbs prior to release. This storing and releasing of energy is what gives an arrow flight.

Mat—Disk of woven straw that holds the target and stops the arrows.

Nock—*n*. The attachment at the rear of an arrow. The nock attachment is then placed on the bow string and this attachment holds the arrow on the string. *v*. To place an arrow on the string.

Nock Point—A mark or device which indicates where the arrow is to be nocked (placed) on the string.

Nylon Mesh Backstop—Nylon material hung in back of targets to stop arrows.

Pinch—Squeezing the index and middle fingers against the nock while drawing the arrow.

Quarrels—see *Bolts*.

Quiver—A satchel, usually worn by the archer, for carrying arrows.

Range—An authorized place for shooting (see *Safety Area*) or the designation for a particular shooting distance.

Recurve Bow—A bow designed so that the ends of the limbs bend away from the archer and curve toward the back of the bow when the bow is held in shooting position.

Release Aid—A device held in a draw hand that acts as a trigger release from the bow string.

Robin Hood—Perhaps the most famous name in archery, especially among non-archers. Robin Hood was the legendary fourteenth-century longbow expert in England's Sherwood Forest.

Round—Units of shooting in an archery contest.

Safety Area—The area around a range which, for safety reasons, is designated off limits during shooting. See *Range*.

Shaft—The arrow, excluding the point, nock and fletching.

Shooting Line—The where the archers stand to shoot. The shooting line runs parallel to the targets.

Shooting Position—The placement of the body when ready to shoot. Not all shooting is done from a standing position. Advanced archers learn to shoot from a prone and a sitting position.

Snapping—A fault in which the archer releases without first sighting and aiming carefully.

Spine—The stiffness of an arrow shaft. The amount an arrow bends is determined by hanging a two-pound weight from the center of the arrow and measuring the bend. This measurement then is used to assign an amount of stiffness to that particular sized arrow.

Stabilizer—A weight attached to the handle riser. A stabilizer is used to minimize the possibility of the archer twisting or rotating the bow while shooting.

Stance—One element of an archer's shooting form; the way in which an archer stands at the shooting line.

Straight-Limb Bow—A bow that is neither recurve nor reflex. When unstrung, this bow lies perfectly flat.

String Silencers—Small rubber attachments to the bowstring to reduce the noise of the bowstring's twang.

String Walking—A technique in which the archer varies the location of his/her nocking point with different shooting distances.

Tab—A flat piece of material which protects the fingers of the drawing hand. Used by more advanced archers. Beginners may find an archery glove easier to handle. See *Glove*.

Tackle—An inclusive term for archery equipment

Takedown Bow—A bow which can be taken apart; especially handy for easy storage or travel.

Target Archery—A form of archery competition in which contestants shoot at large targets from known distances on cleared, level terrain.

Tips—The extreme ends of a bow; the forward most point of an arrow.

Tournament—Organized archery competition.

Toxophilite—A fan or participant greatly devoted to archery.

Traditional Bow—A longbow, similar in appearance to that used by Robin Hood.

Tripods—Target stands.

Tuning—Adjusting the various pieces of tackle—specifically bowstring, arrow rest, and nocking point—to achieve maximum efficiency for an individual's shooting style.

Vanes—Fletching that is made of plastic.

Waiting Line—A line drawn 5.46 yards (5 meters) behind the shooting line. Archers waiting their turn to shoot must remain behind the waiting line.

Wand—A wand shoot is a competitive round for target archers in which the target is a long, narrow, upright slat made of soft wood. The emphasis in a wand shoot is on horizontal accuracy.

United States Olympic Committee
Sports Series Order Form

This unique United States Olympic Committee Sports Series now offers six new titles! Each book is geared toward the beginner but all provide useful information for Olympic fans of all levels. Also, the purchase of these books will help support the U.S. Olympic Team. To order by mail, fax or phone, please use the form below (Please print):

Date:_____

Name: _____

Adress: _____

City:_____State:____Zip: _____

Phone:(_____) _____

Title	Price	Qty / Amount
A Basic Guide to Archery	$7.95	____/_____
A Basic Guide to Cycling	$7.95	____/_____
A Basic Guide to Decathlon	$8.95	____/_____
A Basic Guide to Equestrian	$7.95	____/_____
A Basic Guide to Soccer	$7.95	____/_____
Olympism	$8.95	____/_____

Postage is included   Subtotal: _____

8.25% tax (CA only):   _____

Total: _____

Send this order, with payment (check, money order) enclosed, to:

Griffin Publishing
544 W. Colorado Street
Glendale, CA 91204

For credit card orders, call 818-244-2128 or FAX 818-242-1172

Credit card (circle one)   VISA   MC

Account number _____

Expiration date _____

Signature _____

The National Archery Association of the United States

Benefits of the various NAA membership categories include...

- ◉ Membership in your NAA State Association
- ◉ NAA membership card & decal
- ◉ Subscription to NAA publications
- ◉ Competition & instruction in club program
- ◉ Instructor & coach certification
- ◉ U. S. Archery Team Supporter
- ◉ Leadership opportunities on local, state and national committees and boards
- ◉ Annual state & national rankings
- ◉ Liability insurance
- ◉ Discounts on NAA & USAT items
- ◉ Training camps
- ◉ Event notices & updates
- ◉ "Sport for a lifetime" friendships
- ◉ Opportunity to become a member of the U.S. Archery Teams

NAA Membership Application

Dear NAA Members:

Thank you in advance for your NAA Membership. It helps support the U.S. Archery Team! Please mark the appropriate box for your category of membership below and, when necessary, be sure to fill in the name of your club and any Family, Adult Add-On or Youth Add-on Members!

❏ Adult $32

❏ Youth $15

❏ Collegiate $15

❏ Family $55   Names: _____

❏ Club $50   Name: _____

❏ Adult Add-On $10   Name: _____

❏ Youth Add-On $8   Name: _____

❏ Associate $15

*REMEMBER! You must register one Youth before any Youth Add-On's can join the NAA! Youth Add-On's cannot join with an Adult Member! Thank you.

Name: _____

Address: _____

_____

Phone: (   ) _____

Social Security #: _____

Date of Birth: _____

Return to:
National Archery Association,
One Olympic Plaza,
Colorado Springs, CO 80909